The Little Book of
BIRDS OF
THE WORLD

BUSHEL
& PECK
BOOKS

Published by Bushel & Peck Books, www.bushelandpeckbooks.com.

Bushel & Peck Books is dedicated to fighting illiteracy all over the world.
For every book we sell, we donate one to a child in need—book for book.
To nominate a school or organization to receive free books,
please visit www.bushelandpeckbooks.com.

Type set in Temeraire, Avenir Next, and Bebas.

Illustrations sourced from the Biodiversity Heritage Library. Other image credits as follows:
vine pattern: Nespola Designs/Shutterstock.com; graph paper background:
Vector Image Plus/Shutterstock.com; *Amazona imperialis* by David William Mitchell
via Wikimedia Commons; cover toucan, kiwi, finch, and title page parrot:
The Graphics Fairy; penguin icon: A-spring/Shutterstock.com.
Animal taxonomy sourced from Wikipedia.

ISBN: 9781638190035

First Edition

Printed in the United States

10 9 8 7 6 5 4 3 2 1

The Little Book of
BIRDS OF THE WORLD

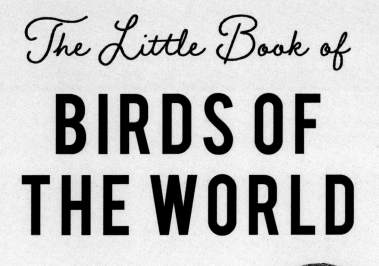

CHRISTIN FARLEY

Contents

SUPERIOR SENSES

With the smallest eyes of any bird species, kiwis have poor eyesight. Thankfully, if kiwis did go blind, their lifestyle would be largely unaffected. They make up for their poor eyesight with their highly developed sense of touch and smell.

1. KIWI

Kiwis are among the world's most unique birds! Found only in New Zealand, they are the pride of their country despite the fact that their tiny wings do not allow them to fly. Like humans, they have marrow in their bones, and they are the only birds with nostrils at the end of their beaks. Kiwis are omnivorous night hunters who walk and probe the ground with their bills in search of insects, seeds, spiders, and plants. Though there are five species of kiwi, they are a shy and elusive species, making it difficult to spot them in the wild.

CLASSIFICATION

KINGDOM: *Animalia*

PHYLUM: *Chordata*

CLASS: *Aves*

INFRACLASS: *Palaeognathae*

CLADE: *Novaeratitae*

ORDER: *Apterygiformes*

FAMILY: *Apterygidae*

GENUS: *Apteryx*

BY THE NUMBERS

50	*lifespan they can reach in years*
20+	*the number of kiwi sanctuaries that exist in New Zealand*
10	*the highest percentage of chicks that reach adulthood*

WEIGHTY MATTERS

Giving birth is no walk in the park for female kiwis. Eggs can grow to be 20% of the mother's mass, putting huge stress on her insides. At the end of pregnancy, she cannot eat since the egg leaves no room for food.

NOT PICKY

If they don't feel like scavenging, marabou storks will seek out their own meals. With stomachs like bottomless pits, they'll eat other birds like flamingos or even shoes and industrial metal parts!

2. MARABOU STORK

While they may not be the most attractive birds, the marabou stork is full of character! A scabby pink face, bald head, large black wings, and skinny legs give it the nickname of "nightmare bird." Life as a scavenger has its advantages. The marabou stork can live pretty much anywhere, though they are commonly found in Africa. Marabou storks are known to follow vultures to good carrion sites and even wait their turn for vulture leftovers. These powerful fliers can reach heights of 13,000 feet, though they spend most of their time close to the ground. Due to their large size, their only predators are large cats like leopards and lions.

CLASSIFICATION

KINGDOM: *Animalia*

PHYLUM: *Chordata*

CLASS: *Aves*

ORDER: *Ciconiiformes*

FAMILY: *Ciconiidae*

GENUS: *Leptoptilos*

SPECIES: *L. crumenifer*

BY THE NUMBERS

12	*wingspan in feet*
5	*the height they can reach in feet*
19	*number of stork species in the world*

STRANGE SAC

The curious sac on the male storks' neck is actually an inflatable sac called a "gular sac." The 18-inch-long appendage stores food and can also puff up in mating season to attract a female.

Harpies have the longest talons of any eagle species at up to four inches in length. That's longer than grizzly bear claws! Applying over 110 pounds of pressure, their talons can easily crush the bones of their targeted prey.

3. HARPY EAGLE

Harpy eagles are powerful, intelligent birds of prey known as "raptors." They make their home in Central and South America in sparsely inhabited areas of the rainforest. Being at the top of the food chain, they feed on monkeys, sloths, and opossums. Harpies have a color combination of black, gray, and white feathers, with facial feathers that they can lift or lower. These monogamous creatures are known for their nest building. Such nests can be 165 feet off the ground and are as large as a double bed. Meticulous builders, they constantly add fresh twigs to keep the nest parasite-free.

CLASSIFICATION

KINGDOM: *Animalia*

PHYLUM: *Chordata*

CLASS: *Aves*

ORDER: *Accipitriformes*

FAMILY: *Accipitridae*

SUBFAMILY: *Harpiinae*

GENUS: *Harpia*

SPECIES: *H. harpyja*

BY THE NUMBERS

1	the number of chicks they raise at a time
25	lifespan in years
2002	the year Panama adopted the harpy eagle as their national bird

POWERLIFTERS

Female harpies are larger than their male counterparts, allowing them to snatch heavier prey. In optimal circumstances, a female harpy can grab and carry prey weighing up to 20 pounds through the air.

Horned
Sungem

Green-
Crowned
Brilliant

HIPPOCAMPUS HELP

A large portion of the hummingbird's brain is taken up by the hippocampus, which is responsible for learning and spatial memory. As a result, hummingbirds remember feeder locations year after year along with flowers they've visited.

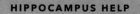

4. HUMMINGBIRD

Found only in the Americas, hummingbirds are versatile and can live in a variety of environments. Only 15 of about 360+ species are found in the U.S., while the vast majority of hummingbirds live in tropical destinations. Ecuador alone has about 130 hummingbird species! Their name comes from the humming noise of their wings as they fly, which beat about 80 times per second. Flexible shoulder joints allow them to fly forward and backward or hover. Due to their heavy physical exertion, hummingbirds need to eat every 10-15 minutes, with nectar being a healthy source of fuel.

BY THE NUMBERS

150	the average number of breaths they take per minute while resting
500	the number of miles a ruby-throated hummingbird can fly non-stop in a day
10	species of hummingbird that are critically endangered

WORLD RECOGNITION

The world's smallest bird is the bee hummingbird. Endemic to Cuba, it only weighs 1.6 grams and is about two inches in length! The largest species is the giant hummingbird at eight inches in length.

Bee Hummingbird

AMAZING RACE

If you race an ostrich, you are sure to lose! As the fastest birds, they can run over 45 mph and can cover 15 feet in one stride! Their speed is aided by their two toes which act like a hoof.

5. OSTRICH

Though flightless and toothless, the ostrich is the world's largest bird. Incredibly powerful legs make up for its lack of flight, with the ability to kill a human or other large predators with its forward kick. Native to Africa's savanna desert, ostriches have the largest eyes of any land animal and the largest eggs of any bird. One ostrich egg is equivalent in size to a dozen chicken eggs! Although they are flightless, these speedy creatures have a use for their wings. Such wings work behind the scenes to keep the ostrich in control and balanced as it zig-zags and runs at high speeds.

CLASSIFICATION

KINGDOM: *Animalia*

PHYLUM: *Chordata*

CLASS: *Aves*

INFRACLASS: *Palaeognathae*

ORDER: *Struthioniformes*

FAMILY: *Struthionidae*

GENUS: *Struthio*

BY THE NUMBERS

330	*average weight in pounds for male ostriches*
2	*weeks they can survive without water*
6.6	*wingspan in feet*

ROCKY DIET

Pebbles are a part of a balanced ostrich diet. Working as a substitute for teeth, the pebbles help break down and grind up plant matter and small reptiles in their gizzards.

Bathing is a regular habit for kingfishers who will clean themselves in nearby water, scrubbing their heads with their wings and even preening their feathers. Their nests are another matter. Nests are known to be a mess heap littered with pellets, droppings, and fish bones.

6. KINGFISHER

It's no mystery, but kingfishers get their name because they are expert fishermen! They are built for the sport with their spear-like beaks and swift, swooping flight patterns. Kingfishers tend to hang out on tree branches near a lake or stream, waiting for the perfect time to dive in after a suitable fish. Brightly colored and medium-sized, kingfishers are characterized by their striking markings and stocky bodies. The distribution of the kingfisher is worldwide, with the greatest variety in tropical areas. Their colors are dependent on their location, but a common combination is black and bright blue feathers with orange bellies.

CLASSIFICATION

KINGDOM: *Animalia*

PHYLUM: *Chordata*

CLASS: *Aves*

ORDER: *Coraciiformes*

SUBORDER: *Alcedines*

FAMILY: *Alcedinidae*

BY THE NUMBERS

28	length in feet of the largest burrow ever built by kingfishers
25	flight speed in mph
10	the largest size of a brood

TEAMWORK

Male and females work together to build their homes. Instead of usual nests, they construct burrows by digging into tree cavities and termite mounds of dirt banks. The process takes about seven days as they take turns digging out soil with their feet.

HOME SWEET HOME

What if there are no barns available for barn owls to nest in? No worries, these owls are resourceful and can make their homes in tree holes, chimneys, church steeples, nesting boxes, and more!

7. BARN OWL

Due to high adaptability, barn owls are found worldwide (except for Antarctica). They can thrive in prairies, deserts, and most wooded habitats. The name "barn owl" comes from their liking of quiet barns on open farmland to build their nests. An added bonus is that such barns often come with their main food source—rodents! Setting them apart from other owl species is their appearance. Barn owls have soft, pale plumage on their face and underparts. Large, dark, beady eyes give them a mysterious look, while females sport more spots on their chests. With sharp talons, these nocturnal hunters are sure to impress!

CLASSIFICATION

KINGDOM: *Animalia*

PHYLUM: *Chordata*

CLASS: *Aves*

ORDER: *Strigiformes*

FAMILY: *Tytonidae*

GENUS: *Tyto*

SPECIES: *T. alba*

BY THE NUMBERS

1,000	the number of rats a family of barn owls can eat a year
14	the largest recorded number of eggs in a brood
1	the average weight of a barn owl in pounds

DEAD OF NIGHT

Barn owls are capable of hunting in complete darkness with their silent flying. Their impeccable hearing also allows them to pick up even the faintest sounds, including locating prey under snow or grass. Such traits make them both skilled and stealthy hunters.

Great Blue
Heron

NEAT AND TIDY

Specialized chest feathers continually grow and fray on the great blue heron to help remove oils and fish slime from their feathers as they preen. As they comb with a claw on their middle toe, this "powder down" acts as a washcloth. The powder down also protects their underparts against oil and slime in swamps.

8. GREAT BLUE HERON

The tall and majestic great blue heron is an excellent fisherman that can be found near bodies of water across North America. While their diet mainly consists of fish, they are not opposed to stalking small mammals and insects. To hunt, they wait patiently for a meal. Once they spot their prey, they will freeze in place, waiting for the right moment to strike with their long, razor-sharp bill. When in flight, it is easy to spot a heron. They fly with their necks tucked in an "S" shape, their legs outstretched and together like an Olympic diver, and their massive grayish-blue wings in graceful motion.

CLASSIFICATION

KINGDOM: *Animalia*

PHYLUM: *Chordata*

CLASS: *Aves*

ORDER: *Pelecaniformes*

FAMILY: *Ardeidae*

GENUS: *Ardea*

SPECIES: *A. herodias*

BY THE NUMBERS

90	*the percentage of their waking time spent stalking food*
4	*approximate height in feet*
6	*weight of an adult in pounds*

NESTING NUMBERS

Colonies of great blue heron are called "heronries," and they are never far from water. Whether on the ground or in trees, a colony can have from 5-500 nests! Nests built in trees can be up to 100+ feet off the ground!

PACK MENTALITY

Family togetherness is a major part of everyday life for red-bearded bee-eaters. They reside with extended families that consist of four overlapping generations. It is believed that they can differentiate between the voices of friends, family, offspring, and nesting neighbors.

9. RED-BEARDED BEE-EATER

"**R**ed-bearded bee-eater" is quite the long title for this medium-sized bird. But like its name, it is far from ordinary! Gorgeously colored, bee-eaters come in almost every color variety, whether they hail from Europe, Australia, or Africa. Vibrant colors are sure to steal your attention along with their slightly curved beaks, slender bodies, and long tail feathers. Depending on their regional environments, their habitats include grasslands, agricultural areas, forests, and savannas. Red-bearded bee-eaters only weigh about two ounces even though they can consume up to 250 bees a day. While beekeepers are not fond of them, red-bearded bee-eaters are a joy to spot in nature!

CLASSIFICATION

KINGDOM: *Animalia*

PHYLUM: *Chordata*

CLASS: *Aves*

ORDER: *Coraciiformes*

FAMILY: *Meropidae*

GENUS: *Nyctyornis*

SPECIES: *N. amictus*

BY THE NUMBERS

8	*average length in inches*
6	*lifespan in years*
27	*number of bee-eater bird species*

WHAT'S IN A NAME

Where does such a name come from? Bee-eaters are actually a bird species known for eating flying insects, particularly bees and wasps. The "red-bearded" part of their name comes from the vermilion (red pigmentation) of their throat feathers.

ORIGINAL BEGINNINGS

In our modern world, hoatzins are known to live in many countries of South America. There is evidence, however, that they may have originated in Europe. Fossil remains similar to hoatzins have been found on the European continent as well as younger fossils in Africa.

10. HOATZIN

The crazy-looking and colorful hoatzins are South American birds known for their strange features. Comparable in size to a pheasant, hoatzins have small, blue, featherless faces; long, separated tail feathers; and an unforgettable spiky crest! Due to underdeveloped chest muscles, hoatzins rarely fly and instead stay local to feed on green plants as exclusive herbivores. You can find them perched near wetlands in shrubs and trees with dense vegetation. Known to be clumsy birds, they like to stick together in colonies. Perhaps this provides added protection against predators like capuchin monkeys.

CLASSIFICATION

KINGDOM: *Animalia*

PHYLUM: *Chordata*

CLASS: *Aves*

ORDER: *Opisthocomiformes*

FAMILY: *Opisthocomidae*

GENUS: *Opisthocomus*

SPECIES: *O. hoazin*

BY THE NUMBERS

26	length in inches of an adult hoatzin
24	height in inches of an adult hoatzin
3	normal number of eggs in a clutch

DIRTY DIGESTION

"Nasty" is a fitting word to describe the hoatzin's digestion. They get the nickname "stinkbird" from the fermentation process that takes place in their crop. This unique digestion gives off an unpleasant and manure-like stench! On the bright side, it does keep them safe from human hunting.

TEMPER TANTRUM

Just like humans, animals can get upset too. Puffins are no exception. They communicate with each other using body language. If a puffin is angry, it may stomp its feet and open its mouth wide.

11. PUFFIN

Often regarded as the cutest birds on Earth, these penguin look-alikes have a short, 10-inch stature, bright orange bills, and fantastic personalities! Puffins may have short wings and stout bodies, but they have the ability to fly as fast as 55 mph as they swoop clumsily from rocky cliffs to the waters below. The majority, or 60%, of puffins breed in Iceland, with most species found in the northern areas of the Atlantic Ocean. Skilled swimmers, puffins use their feet to control their swimming direction and can dive to depths of 60 meters in search of food. Social birds, puffins are noisy talkers in their colonies yet completely silent at sea.

CLASSIFICATION

KINGDOM: *Animalia*

PHYLUM: *Chordata*

CLASS: *Aves*

ORDER: *Charadriiformes*

FAMILY: *Alcidae*

TRIBE: *Fraterculini*

GENUS: *Fratercula*

BY THE NUMBERS

62	record number of fish a puffin caught in its beak at once time!
55	speeds they can fly in miles per hour
3	length of a burrow in feet

PATIENT PARENTING

Male and female puffins are not only dedicated as lifelong partners, but they are also dedicated parents. Each summer, they have one baby that they raise together, feeding it with fish up to 100 times a day. They also dig burrows and even make a toilet area in the front part of the burrow to keep their baby clean.

PREPARE FOR TAKEOFF

Though they have been clocked at flying 60 mph with a tailwind, trumpeter swans average about 30 mph in flight. More important than speed is the need for a clear path for a runway. Swans need at least 100 meters of open water to take off.

28

12. TRUMPETER SWAN

Native to North America, trumpeter swans get their name from their loud honking calls. As the largest member of the continent's waterfowl family, trumpeter swans have wingspans up to 10 feet long and can weigh as much as 35 pounds. Though mostly a majestic white, their entirely black bills and masks set them apart from the similar tundra and mute swans. Sometimes, their heads and necks can have a rust-colored stain. This is due to the minerals in the wetland soil where they feed. Forging strong bonds, males and females will mate for life, building nests in shallow wetlands with abundant food for their young.

CLASSIFICATION

KINGDOM: *Animalia*

PHYLUM: *Chordata*

CLASS: *Aves*

ORDER: *Anseriformes*

FAMILY: *Anatidae*

GENUS: *Cygnus*

SPECIES: *C. buccinator*

BY THE NUMBERS

30	average lifespan in years for trumpeter swans
5	average number of eggs in a clutch
40	percent chance of survival for young swans

NATURAL NUTRITION

If you happen to see a trumpeter swan in the wild, resist trying to feed it. Unlike ducks at a park, swans need to maintain their natural diet of roots and aquatic plants. Feeding swans human food that is rich in protein and calories can contribute to the deformity of their wings.

LOVE BIRDS

Known for being faithful and lifelong mates, mandarin ducks are a symbol of love and fidelity. It is common for newlyweds to be gifted a pair of figurine ducks to aid them in maintaining a healthy marriage relationship.

13. MANDARIN DUCK

Native to China and Japan, the mandarin duck is often regarded as the world's most beautiful duck. This will come as no surprise when you see their splendid plumage, which is depicted widely in local art. Only the male mandarins sport their flashy feathers of many colors; the females exhibit more muted colors of gray and cream, with a white stripe along their faces. Both genders, however, have featherless webbed feet, red bills, and white eye-rings. Mandarin ducks are omnivorous, but their diet can change depending on the time of year. Winter meals consist of plants, while their breeding season diet is made up of fish, worms, snails, and insects.

BY THE NUMBERS

500	distance in miles they can fly in a day
12	the number of eggs in a clutch
12	average lifespan in years of a mandarin duck

FREE FALL

The family nest of the mandarin duck can be as high as 30 feet off the ground. Once ducklings hatch, they must quickly find water. Since they cannot fly shortly after birth, each one leaps from the nest, following its mother's encouraging call from below. Fallen leaves and grass cushion their landing so they remain unharmed.

FLIGHT FATIGUE

In almost constant flight, how do albatross wings not get fatigued? At the base of their wings, albatross have a natural mechanism that keeps their wings "locked" in an extended position. This adaptation eliminates the strain of keeping their wings out.

14. WANDERING ALBATROSS

With the longest wingspan of any bird at an astounding 12 feet, the wandering albatross is sure to catch your eye. You might have to settle for photographs, though, as the wandering albatross inhibits the remote areas of the Antarctic islands. While they spend the majority of their time in the skies, albatross pairs breed and raise their young in frigid climates. Parents switch off feeding their chick with nutritious regurgitated stomach oil. As they mature, the main food sources for wandering albatross are jellyfish, fish, and squid. You can even spot their glistening white forms behind fishing boats, waiting for leftovers.

CLASSIFICATION

KINGDOM: *Animalia*

PHYLUM: *Chordata*

CLASS: *Aves*

ORDER: *Procellariiformes*

FAMILY: *Diomedeidae*

GENUS: *Diomedea*

SPECIES: *D. exulans*

BY THE NUMBERS

26,000	*estimated world population*
1	*the number of chicks born to a pair per year*
12	*the distance away in miles that they can smell food in the water*

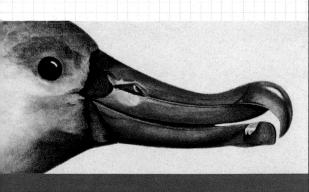

FLIGHT FACTS

Gliding is the key to the albatross' flying success. Without flapping their wings, they can soar through the sky for hours. Extremely efficient, they often use less energy flying than sitting in a nest. On occasion, they have been known to float on water if they cannot fly after gorging themselves on fish.

To cool their bodies, condors exhibit a behavior called "urohidrosis." They poop on their legs which helps to cool them once the excrement evaporates. The downside is that the uric acid stains their legs with a white tinge.

15. ANDEAN CONDOR

Andean condors are vultures who spend their days as scavengers in the Andes mountain ranges of South America. They are characterized by their large, dark bodies, small heads, and white fluff around their necks. Wide-open areas in rocky mountain ranges are their preferred home, where they can easily spot carrion meals. Even though they have an impressive wingspan, condors are not great fliers. Because their weight slows them down, they tend to live in high and windy areas where they can glide instead of fly in the sky. Impressive in stature, they can grow to be four feet in height!

CLASSIFICATION

KINGDOM: *Animalia*

PHYLUM: *Chordata*

CLASS: *Aves*

ORDER: *Accipitriformes*

FAMILY: *Cathartidae*

GENUS: *Vultur*

SPECIES: *V. gryphus*

BY THE NUMBERS

10	pounds of food they can eat in one meal
30	average weight of an adult condor in pounds
125	average gliding speed in miles per hour

ECO FRIENDLY

Andean condors, like all scavengers, play an important role in the health of their ecosystems. By eating dead or decaying animals, they keep their habitats clean and help curb the spread of disease.

CASSOWARY CAUTION

Cassowaries have earned the title of "world's most dangerous bird" for good reason. It is advised to avoid any encounter as they can easily become aggressive. They can deliver slashing and/ or fatal blows with their feet—namely, with their five-inch-long claw on the middle toe of each foot.

16. CASSOWARY

Cassowaries are flightless birds of unusual size native to the tropical rainforests of North Queensland in Australia. Solitary and elusive creatures, cassowaries prefer the tranquil life of basking in dense vegetation while tossing fruit in the air to swallow it whole! As the closest relative of dinosaurs, cassowaries have a unique look. Their stout figure is large like an emu, with a short blue neck; a pointed black beak; a tall, rock-like crest; and sharp toe-claws.

CLASSIFICATION

KINGDOM: *Animalia*

PHYLUM: *Chordata*

CLASS: *Aves*

INFRACLASS: *Palaeognathae*

ORDER: *Casuariiformes*

FAMILY: *Casuariidae*

GENUS: *Casuarius*

BY THE NUMBERS

5	*height in feet they can jump in the air*
50	*egg incubation period in days*
130	*common weight in pounds*

SURPRISING STATS

Did you know that cassowaries are the second heaviest bird in the world (just behind the ostrich)? They are also the third tallest bird in the world behind the ostrich and emu. And lastly, the cassowary egg is the third largest of any bird in the world!

HOME DESIGN

Since bald eagles will use the same nest for years, they continue to add to its size and comfort. While some nests can reach nine feet wide, 20 feet deep, and weigh two tons, more common nests are half that size. They actually hold the record for the largest bird's nest.

17. BALD EAGLE

America's iconic national bird, the bald eagle, is found throughout North America. With vision four to five times stronger than humans, they are the source of the phrase "eagle eyes." Regal in appearance, bald eagles have brown feathers on their body and wings, while their heads and tail feathers are white. Their curved, golden-yellow beaks match their sharp talons. The only thing that doesn't seem to match their majestic stature is their vocal calls. Instead of the piercing screams you might hear in a Hollywood film, bald eagles make an unimpressive, high-pitched giggle call. But we can't be too hard on these birds of prey—they portray a larger-than-life persona!

CLASSIFICATION

KINGDOM: *Animalia*

PHYLUM: *Chordata*

CLASS: *Aves*

ORDER: *Accipitriformes*

FAMILY: *Accipitridae*

GENUS: *Haliaeetus*

SPECIES: *H. leucocephalus*

BY THE NUMBERS

30	*lifespan in years in the wild*
14	*weight in pounds for females (males are smaller at 10 pounds)*
80	*percent of bald eagles who die before reaching adulthood*

SUFFICIENT SWIMMERS

It might be surprising to learn that bald eagles swim! They are known to swoop down to grab a fish out of the water and paddle it to shore using their huge wings in a movement similar to the breaststroke. Hollow bones keep them lightweight while their fluffy down helps with buoyancy.

FATHER FACTOR

Fathers play an important role in the survival of their chick. Once the female lays her softball-sized egg, she sets off for the ocean to feed and gather food. In her absence, the father will cradle the egg for two months, eating nothing. He will lose half his body weight huddling with other dads in the frigid cold.

18. EMPEROR PENGUIN

You just can't help but smile when you see an emperor penguin! Emperors are flightless, but they have an unforgettable waddle! They are also the world's largest penguins. About the size of a six-year-old child, they stand around four feet tall with black backsides and wings. Their front sides are a stark white, with yellow coloring around their necks and a streak of orange on their dark beaks. Emperor penguins are the only animals that live on Antarctica's open ice in the winter. This is why you can often see a large number of penguins huddled together on the ice. Clustering protects them from the howling winds, each member taking their turn on the icy perimeter.

CLASSIFICATION

KINGDOM: *Animalia*

PHYLUM: *Chordata*

CLASS: *Aves*

ORDER: *Sphenisciformes*

FAMILY: *Spheniscidae*

GENUS: *Aptenodytes*

SPECIES: *A. forsteri*

BY THE NUMBERS

600	the depths they can *dive into the* ocean in feet
50	miles they travel each winter to reach breeding grounds
20	lifespan in years in the wild

SMOOTH SWIMMERS

With the ability to hold their breath for 20 minutes underwater, penguins have plenty of time to swim or dive in search of fish, squid, and krill. Their aerodynamic bodies and strong flippers make swimming look effortless.

Yellow-
Casqued
Hornbill

TRIBAL TRIBUTE

Borneo is an island off the coast of Singapore and is home to the indigenous Dayak tribe. Here, hornbills are a symbol of the spirit of God. As a sign of good fortune, hornbills are integrated into the tribe's art, culture, and ceremonial dress.

J.G.Keulemans lith.

Hanhart imp.

19. HORNBILL

If there is something unique for hornbills to boast about, it would be their neck muscles! Their most defining physical feature is their heavy and sizable beak, but the unsung hero is their powerful neck muscles and fused vertebrae which enable them to hold it up. This meaningful member acts like a tool in nest construction, preening, fighting, and fruit-eating. Some hornbills also have an upper part of their beak called a "casque," which is hollow and made of keratin (like our fingernails!). Southeast Asia and Africa are home to these winged wonders. And each species has its own coloration! The closest relatives of hornbills are bee-eaters, kingfishers, and rollers.

CLASSIFICATION

KINGDOM: *Animalia*

PHYLUM: *Chordata*

CLASS: *Aves*

ORDER: *Bucerotiformes*

FAMILY: *Bucerotidae*

BY THE NUMBERS

50+	*number of hornbill species*
150	*the number of figs they can consume in one meal*
8	*weight in pounds of the largest species, the southern ground hornbill*

SECURELY SEALED

After laying her eggs in the hole of a tree, a female hornbill will cover the entrance with mud and droppings, essentially sealing herself inside. She will remain inside, protected from snakes until her chicks are old enough to leave the nest. Her mate gives her food through a small opening in the hole.

When scarlet macaws find themselves in a precarious situation, their first defense technique is to simply fly away. If this option is not available, they are prepared to fight back with their curved beaks, sharp talons, and powerful wings to ward off an offender.

20. SCARLET MACAW

S carlet macaws are famous for their bright plumage of yellow, red, and blue, making them one of the most beautiful members of the parrot family. In their natural habitat of the South American rainforest, the scarlet macaw is perfectly camouflaged from most predators among the vividly colored fruits and flowers. As fairly large birds, macaws can grow to almost three feet in length, though half of that distance is from their long, tapered tail. They are also resourceful and use their beaks as an important tool. Scarlet macaws have no problem using their forceful beaks to crush nuts and seeds or climb trees.

CLASSIFICATION

KINGDOM: *Animalia*

PHYLUM: *Chordata*

CLASS: *Aves*

ORDER: *Psittaciformes*

FAMILY: *Psittacidae*

GENUS: *Ara*

SPECIES: *A. macao*

PET PROBLEMS

While scarlet macaws are highly intelligent and trainable, they are not meant to live alone as pets. They need people around them to keep them company, or they can develop nervous habits like biting or tearing out their own feathers.

BY THE NUMBERS

2	years juveniles stay with their family unit after birth
500–2,000	the pressure generated by their beaks in psi (pounds per square inch)
80	years of age they can reach in captivity, sometimes outliving humans

SURPRISINGLY SOFT

The bill of a toucan is made of bone on the inside, while the outside is constructed of soft keratin. As a result, their bill is not a good tool for fighting or digging, but rather for gathering fruit!

21. TOUCAN

There are about forty species of toucan, and they all share one common trait—their unmistakable bills! Compared to the rest of their bodies, toucan bills are disproportionately large, but they are beautifully colored and show a great deal of variety among the species. Since they are not great fliers, they live in the tree-top canopies of the Central and South American rainforests. Here, they nest in the cavities of trees where they can reach fruit and peel it with amazing dexterity thanks to that recognizable bill. As some of the world's noisiest birds, toucans are more vocal in the afternoon hours. They are also famous for being the national bird of Belize.

CLASSIFICATION

KINGDOM: *Animalia*

PHYLUM: *Chordata*

CLASS: *Aves*

ORDER: *Piciformes*

INFRAORDER: *Ramphastides*

FAMILY: *Ramphastidae*

BORROWED HOME

Groups of toucans like to congregate together on the tops of trees in flocks of 3-12. When it's time to rest, they will go to their borrowed homes of tree cavities made by other birds, the most popular of which is made by woodpeckers.

BY THE NUMBERS

20	average lifespan in years
1963	the year the Toucan Sam became the mascot for Froot Loops cereal
6	tongue length in inches (and it's shaped like a feather!)

IMPRESSIVE EYESIGHT

The vision of peregrine falcons is eight times better than human vision. They can hone in on a target almost two miles away before they dive in for the catch!

22. PEREGRINE FALCON

Outside of Antarctica, peregrine falcons can be found all over the world. As stealthy birds of prey, they can soar long distances by gliding instead of flapping their wings. Peregrine falcons can dive at incredible speeds of up to 242 mph, making them not only the fastest birds on Earth but also highly effective predators. You can recognize these falcons from their black heads, gray plumage, and yellow eye-rings to match their yellow legs and feet. Monogamous, peregrine falcons usually mate for life in their cliff-side nests, laying a clutch of three to four eggs each spring.

CLASSIFICATION

KINGDOM: *Animalia*

PHYLUM: *Chordata*

CLASS: *Aves*

ORDER: *Falconiformes*

FAMILY: *Falconidae*

GENUS: *Falco*

SPECIES: *F. peregrinus*

BY THE NUMBERS

17	*average length of a falcon in inches*
3	*approximate weight in pounds of female falcons (males are slightly lighter)*
21	*the percent of their body weight they must eat a day*

ROUGH BEGINNINGS

Growing up can be difficult for everyone, including peregrine falcon chicks. They are born wet, blind, naked, and completely helpless. It takes about a week for them to gain eyesight and about 30 days to be able to hunt and become independent.

Gouldian Finch

Masked Finch

Long-Tailed Finch

Black-Throated Finch

Masked Finch (White Eared)

PREHISTORIC PRESENCE

Fossil remains have led scientists to believe that true finches have existed on Earth since the Middle Miocene era, which is roughly 10-20 million years ago! Perhaps that is why so many species of finch exist today.

23. FINCH

Adorable songbirds, finches inhabit most areas of the world except for Antarctica, some islands of the Indian Ocean, and the Southern Pacific. Known for their small size, stout bodies, and strong, short beaks, finches come in a variety of color combinations. Most, however, exhibit a brownish base color with hints of red, purple, green, or blue. Finches tend to keep to a vegetarian diet of fruit, nuts, and seeds in their natural habitats of evergreen and tropical forests, as well as in subarctic areas and deserts. As gregarious birds, finches live in "charms" or large flocks where they communicate through their various songs.

CLASSIFICATION

KINGDOM: *Animalia*

PHYLUM: *Chordata*

CLASS: *Aves*

ORDER: *Passeriformes*

SUPERFAMILY: *Passeroidea*

FAMILY: *Fringillidae*

BY THE NUMBERS

650+	*species of finch*
3	*length in inches of the smallest finch, the Andean siskin*
1	*approximate weight of a finch in ounces*

STOUT AND SMART

Bullfinches are known to be shy birds with an amazing vocal gift! If you whistle a tune to them each day for several weeks, they have the uncanny ability to both memorize it and repeat it back to you! Their whistle even sounds like that of a human!

Common
Bullfinch

THE SIMPLE LIFE

"Shy" and "quiet" are fitting adjectives to describe the lyrebird. In some ways, they take after domesticated chickens. They prefer life on the ground and enjoy scratching the dirt with their capable toes and claws in hopes of unearthing insects or seeds beneath the leaf cover.

Superb
Lyrebird

24. LYREBIRD

The southeast coast of Australia is home to lyrebirds whose tall, ornamental feathers resemble the musical instrument called the "lyre." They are unique creatures with the ability to mimic sounds, from a crying baby to a jackhammer or chainsaw. Such an ability is largely due to the fluid-filled cavity in their spinal cord, called a "syrinx," which is the most complex of any bird. Lyrebirds are not big on flying due to their small and weak wings. They spend their days on the ground and climb up in the tree-top canopies of Australia's rainforests by nightfall. Thankfully, such an environment has ample food options such as worms, insects, spiders, centipedes, and seeds.

CLASSIFICATION

KINGDOM: *Animalia*

PHYLUM: *Chordata*

CLASS: *Aves*

ORDER: *Passeriformes*

FAMILY: *Menuridae*

GENUS: *Menura*

BY THE NUMBERS

2.5	*weight in pounds of male lyrebirds*
50	*incubation period in days for lyrebird eggs*
30	*typical lifespan in years*

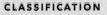

COMFORTABLE COVERAGE

Female lyrebirds take homemaking very seriously. They build cozy, dome-shaped nest structures on the ground, in caves, or even in tree stumps. To make it more comfortable, they will then fill it with moss, roots, feathers, and fern fronds.

NEIGHBORHOOD WATCH

Red-shouldered hawks are one of the main predators of blue jays. When a hawk is spotted, a jay will imitate the sound of its archenemy, therefore alerting other blue jays and neighboring bird species of impending danger.

25. BLUE JAY

Luckily, you don't need to be a bird enthusiast to recognize the loud and intelligent blue jay! Its bright blue plumage (which is not really blue, but an optical illusion) sets it apart from other backyard birds of North America. A pointed black beak, small black eyes, and a black ring around the neck also make its appearance unique. Blue jays are brainy songbirds. They are known by farmers to wait patiently for planting season to swoop down for a lovely feast of seeds. However, blue jays are not picky eaters and will also dine on fruits, berries, acorns, frogs, and insects.

CLASSIFICATION

KINGDOM: *Animalia*

PHYLUM: *Chordata*

CLASS: *Aves*

ORDER: *Passeriformes*

FAMILY: *Corvidae*

GENUS: *Cyanocitta*

SPECIES: *C. cristata*

BY THE NUMBERS

5,000	*number of acorns a blue jay may store during a single fall season*
25	*normal flight speed in miles per hour*
30	*percentage of their body weight they can consume in food each day*

RELATIVE RELATIONS

Did you know that blue jays and crows are related? They both belong to the Corvidae family, and at one point in history, they had a common ancestor. Some of their shared similarities lie in their intelligence, long tails, and strong beaks.

There are many hazards for great white pelicans. Due to overfishing, pelicans have to cover great distances to find food. On top of this, their skin is often turned into leather, while their water pouch is desirable to make tobacco bags. Young pelican fat is also converted to oils in China and India to make traditional medicine.

26. GREAT WHITE PELICAN

Great white pelicans are social animals of Africa's Sahara Desert who live, feed, breed, and migrate in large colonies. Best known for their distinctive bills with large pouches, pelicans are well-equipped for aquatic life. Their bill pouch is stretchy and can hold several liters of water as they scoop fish out of swamps and lakes. Webbed feet and strong legs make pelicans strong swimmers, while their large white and gray wings contribute to their graceful flight.

CLASSIFICATION

KINGDOM: *Animalia*

PHYLUM: *Chordata*

CLASS: *Aves*

ORDER: *Pelecaniformes*

FAMILY: *Pelecanidae*

GENUS: *Pelecanus*

SPECIES: *P. onocrotalus*

BY THE NUMBERS

2 *typical number of eggs females lay each season*

4 *normal breeding age in years*

11 *wingspan length in feet*

FEEDING FRENZY

While fish are a common food choice, great white pelicans are opportunistic feeders. They are not opposed to a meal of chicks from another bird and will also eat turtles, tadpoles, and handouts from humans. If food is scarce, pelicans will even resort to stealing from other birds or eating gulls.

CLEAR THE RUNWAY!

As arctic loons are awkward on land, most of their lives are spent in water. While they are excellent at swimming and flying, they need a good size runway of unobstructed water for flight takeoff.

27. ARCTIC LOON

Also called the black-throated loon, arctic loons are inhabitants of the Northern Hemisphere in parts of Northern Europe and Asia. Regal in appearance, arctic loons have solid black necks with white markings on their black wings. They also have gray hindnecks and heads with white and black stripes on the sides. They can be found in freshwater lakes where waters are calm and peaceful and where crustaceans, fish, and plants are in rich abundance. Bald eagles pose the biggest threat to arctic loons (who have few natural predators). Incubating parents are often susceptible to unsuspecting eagle attacks.

CLASSIFICATION

KINGDOM: *Animalia*

PHYLUM: *Chordata*

CLASS: *Aves*

ORDER: *Gaviiformes*

FAMILY: *Gaviidae*

GENUS: *Gavia*

SPECIES: *G. arctica*

BY THE NUMBERS

7	approximate weight in pounds of adults
5	the number of arctic loon species
2	usual number of eggs in a clutch

DINNER ROUTINE

Sometimes, an arctic loon will have to fly over six miles to find dinner. Once it has come to a body of water, it will dive in 45-second spurts and up to 18-foot depths. Loons use their wings to swim and propel themselves through the water.

EGG WARS

Skua eggs and young are a delicious food source for animals like Arctic foxes, American minks, and glaucous gulls. While that might seem harsh and inhumane, skuas have no problem preying on the eggs of gulls as well.

Great
Skua

28. SKUA

Skuas are not the most hospitable birds; they are known as "jaegers" who pillage and steal from other birds to get their food. For breeding, their home is found in the Arctic tundra, but they migrate to coastal regions of the southern oceans to spend their winter months. Carnivorous and solitary birds, skuas live around 12 years in the wild, only coming on land to breed with their monogamous partners in the summer months. Although they are normally silent avian birds, skuas can communicate using calls. Short calls are made when they are defending their territory or in attack mode. While they can get a bad rap, skuas are charming with their contrasting dark gray and bright white feathers.

CLASSIFICATION

KINGDOM: *Animalia*

PHYLUM: *Chordata*

CLASS: *Aves*

ORDER: *Charadriiformes*

SUBORDER: *Lari*

FAMILY: *Stercorariidae*

GENUS: *Stercorarius*

BY THE NUMBERS

30	*flight speeds they can reach in miles per hour*
95	*the percent of their diet that comes from stealing food in the winter*
1.5	*weight in pounds of adult skuas*

PUFFIN PILLAGING

Unfortunately for the adorable puffins, their breeding time coincides with that of skuas. Being the aggressive bullies that they are, skuas often target puffins to provide much of the nutrients for their newborn brood.

29. CEBU FLOWERPECKER

Decades ago, Cebu flowerpeckers were thought to be extinct before their rediscovery in 1992. Since then, conservation efforts have been a high priority to help reach sustainable numbers of flowerpeckers. Native to Cebu Island in the Philippines, Cebu flowerpeckers thrive in high-humidity and high-temperature parts of the forests. Though they are one of the rarest birds in the world, they are fairly easy to identify. Four hues make up the more colorful males. They sport a white underbelly with black heads, wings, and tail feathers. Their back plumage is a mix of red and tan. Females have a subdued appearance of olive-colored wings and heads.

CLASSIFICATION

KINGDOM: *Animalia*

PHYLUM: *Chordata*

CLASS: *Aves*

ORDER: *Passeriformes*

FAMILY: *Dicaeidae*

GENUS: *Dicaeum*

SPECIES: *D. quadricolor*

BY THE NUMBERS

12	common length in centimeters
48	the number of flowerpecker species worldwide
95	approximate population of Cebu flowerpeckers worldwide

LOST AND FOUND

Zoologist Rob Timmins was the scientist who rediscovered the Cebu flowerpecker after it had last been spotted 100 years prior! What an exciting and celebratory find in the small village of Tabunan.

30. YELLOW-BILLED PINTAIL

Yellow-billed pintails are brown beauties native to many countries of South America. The tops of their heads are dark brown with lighter brown feathers outlined in white. Their vibrant yellow bills are what sets them apart from other pintail species. These ducks are sometimes confused with the yellow-billed teal; the main differences are the pintails' larger size and the black stripe on their bills. Life is spent in wetlands, marshes, and lakes where they thrive on an omnivorous diet of insects and aquatic plants. Yellow-billed pintails are called "dabbling" ducks due to their tendency to dabble in the water instead of dive.

CLASSIFICATION

KINGDOM: *Animalia*

PHYLUM: *Chordata*

CLASS: *Aves*

ORDER: *Anseriformes*

FAMILY: *Anatidae*

GENUS: *Anas*

SPECIES: *A. georgica*

BY THE NUMBERS

20	average length in inches
26	egg incubation period in days
2	number of months chicks are dependent on parents

HIDDEN HIDEOUT

Female yellow-billed pintails take charge of nest building. She will form a nest on the ground hidden in vegetation that is close to the water. Lined with down and grass, her four to ten eggs will be laid here in the hope that predators will not notice them.

HIGHFLIERS

Mallards in flight can reach speeds of 55 mph and tend to soar at altitudes under 10,000 feet. One highflier was recorded as flying at 21,000 feet when it collided with a commercial aircraft, setting an altitude record at the time for bird-aircraft collision.

Mallard

31. MALLARD

Highly versatile, mallards can live in almost any freshwater from North America, Europe, or Asia. This makes them one of the world's most recognized waterfowl, though they typically prefer subtropical and temperate wetlands. Male mallards are highly visible with their characteristic glossy green heads, yellow beaks, and dark brown chests. Females are much less showy, with dull brown, speckled plumage. With a healthy population, mallards are of least concern to animal conservationists even though they have a wide range of predators. Faithful mothers, a female mallard will pretend to be injured in order to distract predators like snakes, raccoons, turtles, and even fish away from her brood.

CLASSIFICATION

KINGDOM: *Animalia*

PHYLUM: *Chordata*

CLASS: *Aves*

ORDER: *Anseriformes*

FAMILY: *Anatidae*

GENUS: *Anas*

SPECIES: *A. platyrhynchos*

BY THE NUMBERS

2/3	portion of their diet that is made up of plants
5	typical life span in years
3.5	weight in pounds of larger mallards

ON THE HUNT

Mallards are one of the most abundant ducks in the world, with an estimated population of over 11 million. This is good news if you enjoy the sport of hunting. Mallards account for one out of every three birds shot for sport in North America, and their numbers are still stable.

AMIABLE ESCORT

Male red-crowned parakeets begin to court their partner two months before becoming a pair. He will escort the female to potential nesting sites and stand guard while she decides if it is suitable. After a site is chosen, the female will prep the site, and her escort will provide food for the two of them.

32. RED-CROWNED PARAKEET

Red-crowned parakeets are small parrots from the island of New Zealand. Most have bright green feathers, but some can display colors of yellow and cinnamon or even feature irregular patches of each. Their name comes from the red patches on the crown of their heads and near their eyes. Old trees are a favorite nesting spot for red-crowned parakeets, but any type of safe cavity is acceptable. Inland, they will forage for fruit, berries, insects, and animal remains. Those parakeets that live in the coastal areas will eat mussels and seaweed. Depending on their diet, the parakeets will also eat tiny stones to help with digestion.

CLASSIFICATION

KINGDOM: *Animalia*

PHYLUM: *Chordata*

CLASS: *Aves*

ORDER: *Psittaciformes*

FAMILY: *Psittaculidae*

GENUS: *Cyanoramphus*

SPECIES: *C. novaezelandiae*

BY THE NUMBERS

7	average egg count in a clutch
20	egg incubation period in days
11	length of adults in inches

BIRTH ORDER

Not all parakeet chicks hatch at once. Some emerge several days after the first. Despite their birth order, each is covered with light gray down and is capable of strong, high-pitched sounds!

FRUITFUL FLOWERS

Do all females like flowers? Male splendid fairywrens hope they do! They are known to collect purple or pink flower petals as part of their courtship display to win over the females.

33. SPLENDID FAIRYWREN

Splendid fairywrens are small and delicate birds of Australia who live active yet non-migratory lives. Males can range from cobalt blue in eastern parts of Australia to violet-blue in the west, with black beaks, eyes, and markings. They make their homes in dry forests or shrublands near acacia and eucalyptus trees. Splendid fairywrens are highly energetic feeders and can be seen hopping and bouncing on the ground as they forage for a wide range of bugs. Fairywrens are not shy and will also frequent backyard bird feeders. When traveling on the open road, keep your eyes alert. Due to their lack of flying strength, fairywrens will often get hit by oncoming vehicles.

CLASSIFICATION

KINGDOM: *Animalia*

PHYLUM: *Chordata*

CLASS: *Aves*

ORDER: *Passeriformes*

FAMILY: *Maluridae*

GENUS: *Malurus*

SPECIES: *M. splendens*

BY THE NUMBERS

2	number of broods fairywrens can produce a year
5.5	common length in inches
11	territory size in acres of woodland areas

RAISING YOUNG

The female fairywren will take the lead when it comes to prepping for a new brood. She builds a small, dome-shaped nest out of bark, roots, and dry grass. After laying her two to four eggs, she takes full responsibility for incubating them for about 15 days.

FADE FACTOR

While some time in the sun is healthy for all, too much can be detrimental. Golden pheasants prefer dense and shadowy habitats, as extended exposure to sunlight can fade their brilliant colors.

34. GOLDEN PHEASANT

Golden pheasants are exotic and flashy birds that are native to China's mountain ranges. Males' spectacular plumage incorporates many colors such as red, blue, green, purple, orange, and a bright golden yellow on their heads. While they might sound like tropical birds, their extensive tails set them apart from other bird species. In fact, their tail makes up two-thirds of their entire body length! Females are not nearly as eye-catching with their dull brown plumage and smaller size. Such differences make it easy to tell the genders apart. Similarly to chickens, you can find pheasants feeding all day long on the ground for grains, leaves, and insects. At night, you will find them roosting in trees.

GOOD LUCK CHARM?

In Chinese culture, golden pheasants are a sign of good luck and prosperity. It is also believed by some that if you catch a golden pheasant, you can have three of your wishes granted!

CLASSIFICATION

KINGDOM: *Animalia*

PHYLUM: *Chordata*

CLASS: *Aves*

ORDER: *Galliformes*

FAMILY: *Phasianidae*

GENUS: *Chrysolophus*

SPECIES: *C. pictus*

BY THE NUMBERS

12	*eggs female golden pheasants can lay in a clutch*
44	*inches in length of male golden pheasants*
1.2	*weight in pounds of the small game bird*

Goldie's Bird-of-Paradise

LOUD AND PROUD

Birds-of-paradise are audacious and loud birds that seem to be constantly vocal. Males combine their elaborate mating dances with song, while calls and sounds are also made to mark territories and alert others of impending danger.

35. BIRD-OF-PARADISE

Members of the Paradisaeidae family, birds-of-paradise come in many varieties and are predominantly found in New Guinea and its surrounding islands. Almost all nest in trees and feed on fruits and small insects. Their defining characteristics are their brightly colored ornamental feathers. Bird-of-paradise species exhibit sexual dimorphism, where males have vibrant plumage compared to the drab appearance of females. Some male species have elongated feathers (known as "streamers" or "wires"), large head plumes, and other distinctive ornaments like head fans and breast shields. Such feathers come into play during their complex courting rituals.

CLASSIFICATION

KINGDOM: *Animalia*

PHYLUM: *Chordata*

CLASS: *Aves*

ORDER: *Passeriformes*

SUPERFAMILY: *Corvoidea*

FAMILY: *Paradisaeidae*

BY THE NUMBERS

42	*number of bird-of-paradise species*
7	*years it takes males to develop their beautiful plumage*
1522	*the year birds-of-paradise first appeared in European literature*

SOCIAL STATUS

Feathers of birds-of-paradise have had many uses over the centuries. Culturally, plumes have been symbols of power, wealth, and status, and have even been used as currency by certain New Guinea tribes.

Blue Bird-of-Paradise

While they tend to travel in fairly small groups, imperial amazons are never found alone. Three is a normal-sized group, but, occasionally, they will mix and form small colonies with other breeds like the red-necked amazon.

36. IMPERIAL AMAZON

If you ever get the chance to see an imperial amazon in the wild, make sure to snap a picture, as you might not have another opportunity! These parrots are only found on the Caribbean island of Dominica and are critically endangered, with populations only in the hundreds. Imperial amazons thrive in rainforest canopies and mountain forests with plentiful fruits, nuts, and vegetables for their herbivorous diet. These rare beauties sport gorgeous plumage of purple, green, and blue, giving them a distinct and recognizable appearance. Long living and monogamous birds, imperial amazons are shy yet fascinating creatures!

CLASSIFICATION

KINGDOM: *Animalia*

PHYLUM: *Chordata*

CLASS: *Aves*

ORDER: *Psittaciformes*

FAMILY: *Psittacidae*

GENUS: *Amazona*

SPECIES: *A. imperialis*

BY THE NUMBERS

19	*length in inches*
55	*average life expectancy in years*
2	*weight in pounds*

LOW NUMBERS

There are a number of factors that contribute to the low population of imperial amazons. One is their low reproduction rate. Chicks are born every other year in small clutches of one to two eggs. Hurricanes can also cause destruction to life and habitat, requiring imperial amazons to spend many years reaching their former numbers.

SUPERIOR STRUCTURES

Kagus are the only bird species to have "nasal corns." These structures cover their nostrils and are believed to keep soil and debris from entering their noses while rooting through the soil for insects and worms to eat.

37. KAGU

Endemic to the New Caledonia islands of the South Pacific, kagus are rare, flightless birds with pearl-gray feathers, red eyes, and long, red legs. Similar in size to a chicken, they make their nests out of sticks and leaf litter on the ground of the dense forests. Unlike most flightless birds, kagus have full-sized wings that serve multiple purposes. Like arms, kagu wings allow them to move quickly through the forest and keep their balance while hopping and climbing over rocks. A kagu parent may also flap its wings on the ground in hopes of appearing injured to distract predators away from its chick.

CLASSIFICATION

KINGDOM: *Animalia*

PHYLUM: *Chordata*

CLASS: *Aves*

ORDER: *Eurypygiformes*

FAMILY: *Rhynochetidae*

GENUS: *Rhynochetos*

SPECIES: *R. jubatus*

BY THE NUMBERS

1	*the number of eggs in a clutch*
2	*average weight in pounds*
25	*typical lifespan in years*

CULTURAL ICON

The survival of the kagu is vital to the people of New Caledonia. Kagus' early morning song has been recorded and is played by the islanders each night as their territory's national song. This high-profile bird brings good luck and a good economy to the area.

A kagu egg

ONE OF A KIND

As far as global distribution goes, spoonbills are found on every continent with the exception of Antarctica. One specific species of the African spoonbill can only be seen in Africa and Madagascar. You can tell it apart from other spoonbills by its red face and legs.

38. SPOONBILL

Wading and foraging in shallow waters are two favorite pastimes for aquatic spoonbills. They prefer the freshwater habitats of wetlands, marshes, lakes, and ponds where they use their specialized bills to hunt. In fact, it is their long, flat, spoon-shaped bills that earned them their namesake! With a side-to-side motion of their bills in the muddy waters, spoonbills feel for small fish, shrimp, insects, crabs, and plants to snatch up. While they are more abundantly seen with white plumage, black bills, and black feet, the popular roseate spoonbill comes in pale pink and dark magenta hues.

CLASSIFICATION

KINGDOM: *Animalia*

PHYLUM: *Chordata*

CLASS: *Aves*

ORDER: *Pelecaniformes*

FAMILY: *Threskiornithidae*

SUBFAMILY: *Plataleinae*

GENUS: *Platalea*

BY THE NUMBERS

6	*number of spoonbill species*
30	*common height in inches*
6	*age in weeks before chicks can fly on their own*

NEIGHBORLY NEIGHBORS

Spoonbills are peaceful and social birds that nest in colonies. They will gather with other like-minded water waders like gray herons and glossy ibises. In addition, they are known to have social circles wide enough to welcome storks, egrets, and cormorants.

FILTER FEEDERS

Greater flamingos are omnivorous feeders that stir up the shallow waters with their webbed feet. To feed, they sweep their beaks upside down in the water, and a filter structure in their bills removes the food particles before draining the water.

39. GREATER FLAMINGO

As the largest of the flamingo species, greater flamingos are easily recognized from their large, crooked bills and bright-pink plumage. They are the only flamingos that are found outside of North and South America, instead inhabiting the Middle East, Africa, and Southern Europe. Mostly found in shallow bodies of saltwater, greater flamingos have special scales on their legs and feet to protect them from the potentially harmful effects of prolonged saltwater exposure. Their only use for freshwater is for bathing and drinking. A favorite for kids and adults alike, you can often see them standing on one leg in their social surroundings with others of their kind.

CLASSIFICATION

KINGDOM: *Animalia*

PHYLUM: *Chordata*

CLASS: *Aves*

ORDER: *Phoenicopteriformes*

FAMILY: *Phoenicopteridae*

GENUS: *Phoenicopterus*

SPECIES: *P. roseus*

BY THE NUMBERS

5	*height in feet of adults*
8	*common weight in pounds*
10	*average flamingo count in a colony*

PRETTY PIGMENT

What causes flamingos to have such lovely pink coloring? Is it something they are born with? No! Flamingos are actually born white and gray and develop their pink coloring at around age two. Their pink pigment comes as a result of their crustacean diet.

NASTY NOURISHMENT

If dead and decaying animals weren't disgusting enough, Egyptian vultures are also known to eat poop! Excrements of humans and other large animals provide vultures with added nourishment that helps to stabilize their face-coloring.

40. EGYPTIAN VULTURE

Egyptian vultures differ from other vulture species in their appearance. Their beautiful, brilliant, white plumage compliments their black underwings and yellow, featherless faces. They thrive as the smallest of all vultures in arid plains and roost in the tall trees of North Africa and India. Similar to many species, Egyptian vultures eat carrion and other rotting foods. Bird eggs are also a popular food choice, as they are skilled enough to use stones to crack open eggs that are particularly hard-shelled. Mostly solitary animals, vultures are active daytime hunters who prefer to spend their winter months in the warmer Sahara Desert.

CLASSIFICATION

KINGDOM: *Animalia*

PHYLUM: *Chordata*

CLASS: *Aves*

ORDER: *Accipitriformes*

FAMILY: *Accipitridae*

GENUS: *Neophron*

SPECIES: *N. percnopterus*

BY THE NUMBERS

30	*average lifespan in years*
2	*normal count of eggs in a clutch*
80	*travel distance in miles when searching for food*

HISTORIC HIEROGLYPHICS

Egyptian vultures are depicted in ancient Egyptian hieroglyphics most likely for their cleverness. Perhaps this is where they got the nickname "Pharaoh's chicken." They were also worshiped as a symbol of the Goddess Isis.

ABOUT THE AUTHOR

Christin is the author of several books for kids, including many in the Little Library of Natural History. She lives with her family in California, where she enjoys rollerblading, puzzles, and a good book.

**BUSHEL
& PECK
BOOKS**

ABOUT THE PUBLISHER

Bushel & Peck Books is a children's publishing house with a special mission. Through our Book-for-Book Promise™, we donate one book to kids in need for every book we sell. Our beautiful books are given to kids through schools, libraries, local neighborhoods, shelters, nonprofits, and also to many selfless organizations who are working hard to make a difference. So thank you for purchasing this book! Because of you, another book will find itself in the hands of a child who needs it most.